The Emperor's New Clothes: A Contemporary Business Life Edition

By: Ade Asefeso, Steffen Brygger Lund & Hadrian Parry

Illustrations: Otso Iho

Second Edition

Copyright 2014 by: Ade Asefeso, Steffen Brygger Lund & Hadrian Parry. All rights reserved.

ISBN-13: 978-1500701048

ISBN-10: 1500701041

Publisher: AA Global Sourcing Ltd
Website: http://www.aaglobalsourcing.com

Table of Contents

Preface 5
Disclaimer 7
Dedication 8
Chapter 1: Introduction 9
Chapter 2: Transformational Change 15
Chapter 3: Why it is Difficult to Implement Transformational Change 21
Chapter 4: Are Management Fads the Emperor's New Clothes? 27
Chapter 5: Dealing with the Emperor's New Clothes 33
Chapter 6: Examples of Failed IT Projects 41
Chapter 7: Leadership Lessons from the Emperor's New Clothes 45
Chapter 8: Employee Engagement 49
Chapter 9: Variety of Employee Enabling Activities 55
Chapter 10: Information Sharing 63
Chapter 11: Using Fair Process to Build Trust 71
Chapter 12: Using Mistakes as an Opportunity for Learning 77
Chapter 13: Learning from Children 81
Chapter 14: Avoid the Dangers of Management Babbles 89
Chapter 15: All Good Fairy Tales Come to an End with a Memorable Moral 95

Other Book from the same Authors 101

Preface

This book is about friendship, believing in one another and a drive to challenge the status quo of the established business world. The journey leading to this book started 10 years ago when the 3 of us met at a little village on the outskirts of Oxford in England, United Kingdom, at a strategy residential related to our MBA studies.

After finalizing our MBA studies and despite busy careers in different parts of the world, we continued to keep in close and frequent contact .As a result of our numerous discussions over the years and sharing ideas from our different business practices, the idea for this book slowly emerged.

As active business practitioners, we experienced so many "corporate change initiatives" that despite being launched with a lot of "rah-rah" and backed by world-class consultants were at best leading nowhere. We also saw the emergence of "Power Point Fatigue," creeping into all meeting rooms in our daily work. It seemed that the more colourful, data-rich and animated slides you could produce, the more convincing you were. We saw the "Fatigue" hitting the organizations we work with and found great relief in the famous quote by Steve Jobs: "You only need Power Point slides when you don't know what you are talking about." This is where our fairy tale and the art of storytelling come into the picture.

Despite being an emerging discipline in the study of management strategy and organization studies, we are firm believers in "Organizational Storytelling." Replacing an endless number of Power Point slides, storytelling can be a powerful tool to connect colleagues to your ideas and help them make sense of the world around them. Fairy tales and stories stick. The characters and motifs of fairy tales like "The Emperor's New Clothes" by Hans Christian Andersen are simple. Once told, you remember the story and the deep and profound moral for the rest of your life.

This book is not a fairy tale itself. However, with an offset in "The Emperor's New Clothes," it draws parallels between the characters, motifs, and moral of this famous fairy-tale and today's business world. It is our hope that you as a reader will recognize the "Emperor," "Weaver," "Child" and "Father" in yourself. It is also our hope that in the future more business people will find the courage to speak up when they see "nakedness" in any proposed business initiative.

Disclaimer

This publication is designed to provide competent and reliable information regarding the subject matter covered. However, it is sold with the understanding that the authors and publisher are not engaged in rendering professional advice. The authors and publishers specifically disclaim any liability that is incurred from the use or application of the contents of this book.

There are a number of morals that you can get from "The Emperor's New Clothes." One of the most obvious ones is that people should articulate what they feel and should have their own views; the content of this book is our view and it does not represent what is happening in all organisations out there and as such, our suggested solutions are simply our own views.

Look before you leap. Sometimes innocent children can see things more clearly than adults. Don't believe everything you're told by those who seek gain. Don't assume others are right simply because you perceive their status to be higher than yours as we are not claiming that our suggestions in this book are the only solutions to the subject matter. If you purchased this book without a cover you should be aware that this book may have been stolen property and reported as "unsold and destroyed" to the publisher. In this case neither the authors nor the publisher have received any payment for this "stripped book."

Dedication

To the brave Child of today's corporate world.

Chapter 1: Introduction

When we were kids, we were given the Hans Christian Andersen, 1837 story book, 'The Emperor's New Clothes'. We used to think the story was really funny, but as we grew up, we realized that 'The Emperor's New Clothes' had a profound moral.

The story was about an Emperor who cares only about his looks. One day, two scoundrels pretending to be weavers promise to make him a suit from a beautiful fabric that happens to be invisible to anyone who is stupid or incompetent. The Emperor is so impressed by the weavers' 'sales talk' that he hires them to make the suit. Though the Emperor cannot see the cloth himself, he pretends that he can because he does not want to appear stupid. All his ministers and court staff do the same.

When the swindlers report that the suit is finished, he pays them in gold and they pretend to dress him using mime. The Emperor then marches in procession before his subjects.

A child in the crowd sees the Emperor in his underwear and shouts that the Emperor is wearing nothing at all. The child's father tells him to shut up but many others in the crowd also notice.

The Emperor realizes the truth but thinks it better to continue with the procession. He thinks it is better that the public appear stupid for not being able to see the special cloth than for him to appear stupid for appearing naked!

The moral of this story

If something does not look right, sound right or feel right to you no matter how many authoritative figures claim that it is true, research the issue and make up your own mind.

When applied to corporate life

1. **The Emperor symbolizes Government, CEOs and Top Managers.**

Some Government, CEOs and Top Managers spend a lot of time looking good, showing off vis-à-vis their many stakeholders (tax payers, peers, employees, board members, shareholders, media etc). Other Government, CEOs and Top Managers are more focused on creating results and getting the job done, i.e. they spend time "at court" and less focused on how they are perceived by their many stakeholders mentioned above. Which one are you?

2. Weavers 1 and 2 symbolize consultants and experts.

We are all surrounded by "the finest solutions to our challenges." Consultants and experts are ready to step in and help the Government, CEOs and Top Managers. They normally show them a repository of the best references from companies and countries they have helped so far. But why do Government, CEOs and Top Managers need "weavers" to make it right? What are their motives for engaging expensive consultants and experts? Don't they know the answers themselves or do they just need consultants to justify decisions they have already made? Do they really need consultants to identify the "incompetent and stupid" parts of their organizations?

By drawing on the authors' experiences and discussions with numerous senior managers across a wide range of industries, we hope to provide answers to all of the above questions in this book!

3. Ministers symbolize some of the media and middle managers.

Some Governments, CEOs and Top Managers want to be perceived as following the most recent fashion in management theory. They use consultants or large scale projects to identify the "fit" or "unfit" parts of their organization. Such initiatives are normally costly exercises and often disrupt the daily work of the company or Government Departments. Furthermore, despite tough financial challenges there is always enough money for such projects. Consultants often present the projects as "hard night and day work," but the effort that really goes into the project is seldom transparent. Despite the fact that the media and middle managers can often clearly see that the emperor is naked, some go along with the spin and strengthen the illusion that the emperor has a new clothe!

4. Court Staff symbolizes Stakeholders, such as Employee and Pressure Groups.

Often the progress of these projects is rather intangible. People are sceptical of where the project will take them but as the project is initiated by top management and often involves world class management consultancies, it is hard to speak up and express your scepticism. Even though you realise something is wrong, a little voice in your head tells you: "maybe I am the stupid one who cannot see the broader picture." Many such projects also involve the individual employees and pressure groups, and since they did not express their scepticism upfront it becomes more and more difficult to do at later stages as the project is implemented. Passive aggression becomes the norm and nobody has the courage to declare publicly that the "the emperor is naked!"

Many of these projects are relatively costly exercises and often consume much more resources than anticipated, whether measured in money, time or emotional stress. More often than not, the additional required resources are found as there seems to be "no way back". By this point, the top management is locked in a 'vicious circle.' The more they invest the harder it gets to admit that the project is "The Emperor's New Clothes." Many such projects more or less involve the whole organization, and as more people get involved and fail to speak up, the harder it gets to do so because their little voices keep sowing doubt in their mind, saying, "Maybe it is only me who is stupid or incompetent."

These projects always consume an enormous amount of resources and it is really hard to evaluate what happens behind the scenes. Many consulting firms do present impressive Power Point presentations showing how complex the proposed project is. They insert your company name on all slides but occasionally most of these materials are actually "re-used material" from previous clients. Nonetheless, they pretend to work night and day, just for YOU!

5. The Child symbolizes us and other people who see the truth.

Finally, a young boy looked up at the emperor, saw the truth, and shouted out; "The emperor has no clothes!" How many people today are prepared to be the young boy and save our country or organisation a lot of money and management time on a project that could potentially bring a country or a corporation down?

6. The Father symbolizes our family, colleagues and close friends who disbelieve.

In the original story, the boy's father grabs him and says "Don't talk nonsense!" He whisks the boy away in just the same way our friends and colleagues will ask us not to speak out in fear of losing our jobs; jobs that could potentially be lost anyway if the project fails.

7. The Public symbolizes everyone else.

In the original story, everyone who heard the boy begins to admit the emperor is naked, raising a murmur from the crowd; "The boy is right! The emperor has no clothes! It's true."

We decided to use this book to address some world issues and corporate practices that did not seem right to us and express our ways of thinking differently and seeing the facts in a different light.

Chapter 2: Transformational Change

Sometimes it seems that most change management initiatives on transformational change are similar to the story of The Emperor's New Clothes.

If you are not familiar with the classic fairy tale by Hans Christian Andersen, it is the story of two weavers who promise the Emperor that they will create a splendid new set of clothes for him. The problem is that the clothes are never actually produced, yet everyone around the Emperor comments on the beauty of the clothing despite the fact that they do not exist.

Risk Averse Organizations are like The Emperor Has No Clothes in that the clothes are "invisible." Finally a young boy proclaims the truth: "The Emperor has no clothes!" So many organizations today are trying to implement transformational change in the face of risk-averse cultures where it is not okay to speak the truth. But if we are looking to transform the organization, we have to begin by speaking the truth and acknowledging our past failures! Frankly, that acknowledgement is a powerful first step. In fact, some of the most successful transformations we have seen during our corporate days have been those where the sponsor has been totally transparent and ready to admit that he has no clothes (that he or she is in fact naked) and ready to engage people across the organisation, giving them the freedom to speak freely and run the change management program from bottom up rather from top down.

When the Sponsor of the transformational change acknowledges that the transformation is going to be painful for everyone, including the leaders, and makes the journey transparent, it sends a very important message to the whole organization.

Too often, though, leaders mistakenly assume that the transformation will have little impact on their world. Or, as one of the Senior Managers of an organization we are familiar with put it, the leaders like to "admire the problem" rather than speak the truth about what needs to change, including what they need to change about themselves and the difficult choices they need to make that impact them personally.

Very often organizational change is met by resistance. Such a resistance is the natural part of any organization's DNA, and therefore any sponsor of a successful transformational change must engage and involve those in the organization affected by the proposed change. The more they involve the organization in "designing the Emperor's New Clothes," the more successful the initiative will be.

It is ironic that our failure to speak the truth and let everyone know that "the Emperor has no clothes" only increases resistance and slows down the transformational change.

So what can we do differently to change this pattern and save the time and energy we spend on finding ways to avoid acknowledging the truth that the Emperor has no clothes?

We have found in our own change management initiatives that it is extremely important to provide leaders with some education and awareness around their role in the transformation process. Important messages to consider includes:

- They control the pace of the implementation of the transformation, not the Change Agents.
- Successful transformational change requires radical changes to their own behaviour as Sponsors; minor adjustments won't be enough.
- The transformational change must be seen as personally painful to the Sponsors.
- The transformation must be a top priority for a considerable period of time.
- The more transparency the sponsors demonstrate, the more effective the psychological cues that suggest the transformation represents a break from the past.
- Effective sponsors should be good "storytellers," capable of painting a clear and compelling picture of how the future will look after the change initiative.
- Sponsors who acknowledge past failures openly also provide powerful psychological cues.

Sponsors at the highest levels must also "begin the cascade of demonstrated commitment" to the transformation with their own direct reports. This commitment includes what the sponsors say, what they do, and what they reinforce; all three of these behaviours need to be aligned around the new organizational values. The sponsors must be willing to demonstrate truthfulness and accountability with their own direct reports if the organization is going to overcome a risk-averse culture.

When what the Sponsors say, do, and reinforce get out of sync, levels of trust plummet and resistance to the transformation goes up. When the level of trust decreases, it just takes more resources and takes longer to realise the value of the desired transformational change.

Numerous organizations today seek transformational change as a requirement of a rapid and constantly changing environment. If everyone continues to trudge along afraid to speak the truth about what needs to be different, we will fall into the same traps we have faced in the past.

The young boy in the fairy tale can teach us a lesson or two about transformation. If the whole organization is involved and engaged in designing and producing the Emperor's New Clothes, they will appreciate the outcome of all their mutual efforts and they will honestly proclaim; "What a wonderful fit," "What a pattern," "What colours," "Such luxurious clothes!"

In our opinion, clothes made of the best materials and manufactured by the most professional and honest tailors always last longer. The same goes for organizational transformation initiatives.

Chapter 3: Why it is Difficult to Implement Transformational Change

This chapter is a review of early and current trends in strategic thinking and the possibilities emerging from developments in the field of change management and decision support systems.

The business world has been subjected to fundamental structural transition brought about by deregulations, global competition, and technological discontinuities over the past decade. This has resulted in new customer expectations and imposed new strains on business managers. In attempts to restore the competitive edge, many managers are abandoning old strategy recipes and looking for new and more effective guidance to help them navigate in turbulent environments. Yet, are these recipes really new or are they just the emperor's new clothes?

As we head toward a post-industrial society we need new concepts of the world to orient ourselves. Classical concepts have become unreliable and, what is worse, to some extent even irrelevant; in our opinion, is not so much the rules that have changed, but it is the game that is starting to resemble the adventures of Alice in Wonderland; therefore we invite all corporate elephants to learn how to dance to the tunes!

In recent years, many corporate change activists have been exposed to principles, tools and practices loosely referred to as "transformational." Many trainers, facilitators, consultants, coaches and other intermediaries use the word in their work, and there is a growing field of "corporate transformation." This term and field actually encompass a wide range of approaches, and there is as yet no agreement about what is and what is not considered "transformation."

In our opinion, it is useful to think of transformational change as profound, fundamental and irreversible. It is a metamorphosis, a radical change from one form to another.

Transformation is an approach, a philosophy and a methodology. The following is an initial attempt to articulate some of the key principles that seem to underlie much of the work being done in this field.

The terms "transformational change" and "transformation" may be two of the most over-used words in business today. In our change management initiatives, we identify three different types of strategic change:
1. **Minor change** creates minimal disruption (and therefore minimal resistance to change). Examples are routine changes to policies and procedures.
2. **First order change** creates significant disruption so there is consequently also major resistance to change. An example is a new Enterprise Resource Planning (ERP) system like Oracle, SAP, Microsoft Dynamics etc. or the introduction of a portfolio management tool.

3. **Second order change** is "transformational change" and is a complete alteration of the current operating structure, with massive change to organizational silos, processes, people, and typically, technology. Since resistance is a function of the level of disruption the change creates, transformational change also brings with it significant resistance. An example of second order changes is the adoption of shared services solutions that break down organizational silos and drastically alter how the company operates.

Based on our observations of change management initiatives, we can predict at least 10 common barriers to transformational change:

1. Lack of clear scope/definition: An amazing number of organizations embark on the transformational change journey with no clear, consistent definition of where they are going. Leaders have multiple, often conflicting agendas. They want to dress nicely like the Emperor but are not sure about the type of clothes they want.

2. Too many other changes competing for resources: Senior executives routinely underestimate the level of resources needed for transformational change. "Implementation" is a ferocious, resource consuming activity. Once the strategy is designed you are only 15% of the way to transformation! You still have 85% of the journey ahead. The best advice is to; focus on the key 20% that will deliver 80% of the solutions required.

3. Poor implementation history: If your organization has a cemetery full of "dead and buried" projects, you can expect the memories of these to linger on. You will likely face resistance to your current transformational change based on the experience of previous failed projects. If you have seen the Emperor naked several times it is hard to believe that his next fashion show will be any better.

4. No sustained leadership support: Sponsorship for the transformation will need to be sustained for a considerable period of time. It is easy to get distracted and to divert precious resources before the transformation is fully complete. You can also predict that over the course of this time that there will be major changes in leadership and you will need to begin from "square one" in securing sponsorship from these new leaders. Plan for that upfront!

5. Major employee resistance: Since resistance is a function of disruption, we know that transformational change will result in major levels of resistance. You need to have a plan for how that resistance will be dealt with and managed. Don't expect that you can communicate your way out of resistance. If all you do is communicate, you will likely just generate more resistance. If the Emperor is naked he is naked!

6. Weak motivation: The motivation to leave the current state must be greater than the desire to stay where you are. Transformation will happen only when the tension between what is and what should be gets big enough. The only way to motivate people is to alter the reinforcements. One of the biggest mistakes organizations make is to apply the same type of reinforcements (both formal and informal) while expecting transformational changes in behaviour.

7. Risk-averse cultures: If your culture is one where turf-guarding is the political norm, you can anticipate that transformational change will fly in the face of your culture. Unless there are radically different reinforcements instituted for sponsors (for example, reinforcement for mutual success rather than individual success) your transformation is at risk.

8. Poor communications: Pay attention to the psychological cues you are giving in your delivery methods. If the standard operating method is email, for example, you will need to demonstrate that you are working toward radical change by your choice of media. You will not get people's attention by just adding to the volume of email traffic and communicating from the 70,000th foot of the corporate ladder. Adding colourful Power Point slides will not do the job either; radical change requires radical communication methods.

9. Unclear and/or undisciplined governance structure: How will the transformation be managed? If you are creating "enterprise-wide" change you cannot have multiple approaches with no oversight on how the entire program is being managed. The governance structure should provide a clear line of sight from strategy to portfolio to programs, projects, and sub-projects. If Sponsors do not have this line of sight then the transformational change portfolio will lack disciplined management.

10. Use of multiple approaches reinforces the silo mentality: How you implement is important! Our experience tells us that for significant change management initiatives you must always begin with the end in mind. If you are trying to break down silos, it is totally paradoxical to implement change in a silo'ed manner. Finally, please speak up if you see the Emperor is naked during any transformational initiative. The process should be stopped before the Emperor embarrasses himself and his whole court!

Chapter 4: Are Management Fads the Emperor's New Clothes?

Management fad is a term used to characterize a change in philosophy or operations implemented by a business or institution.

The term is subjective and tends to be used in a pejorative sense, implying that such a change is being implemented (often by management on its employees, with little or no input from them) solely because it is (at the time) "popular" within managerial circles, and not necessarily due to any real need for organizational change. The term further implies that once the underlying philosophy is no longer "popular," it will be replaced by the latest "popular" idea, in the same manner and for the same reason as the previous idea and like with clothes and fashion, the new fads come and go.

Several authors have argued that new management ideas should be subject to greater critical analysis, and for the need for greater conceptual awareness of new ideas by managers.

Management fads are often characterized by the following:

- New jargon for existing business processes.
- External consultants who specialize in the implementation of the fad. A certification or

appraisal process performed by an external agency for a significant fee.
- Amending the job titles of existing employees to include references to the fad.
- Claims of a measurable business improvement via measurement of a metric that is defined by the fad itself.
- An internal sponsoring department or individual that gains influence due to the implementation of the fad.
- Big words and complex phrases.
- Evidence that a given fad works in real life is often scarce and often only based on anecdotes or fairy tales.

Examples of Management Fads

The following theories and practices appeared on a list of management fashions and fads compiled by us and we arranged them in rough chronological order by their date of appearance, from the 1950s to the 1990s:

- Management by objectives
- Matrix management
- Theory Z
- One-minute management
- Management by wandering around
- Total quality management (TQM)
- Business process reengineering
- Delayering
- Empowerment
- 360-degree feedback
- Re-engineering
- Teamwork

Other theories and practices which we tagged as fads include:
- Deming system
- The customer service revolution
- Knowledge management
- Six Sigma
- ISO 9000
- Best Practices
- 5S (methodology)
- Kaizen

- Capability Maturity Model Integration
- Quality circles
- Agile

For the purpose of this chapter we shall look into some of the above management fads.

If for example Lean Six Sigma manufacturing works so well, why aren't there as many successful Lean Six Sigma companies as there are successful Lean Six Sigma consultants? Following 35 years of application we still only speak of a select few who are sustainably Lean! Toyota, Nissan, the usual examples. For the majority of companies the reported improvements are not sustained over time, provoking the industry at large to use terms like "culture" to enable blame to be apportioned to some non-entity that hasn't really understood this "loose talk". This disassociates people from responsibility and business continues as usual.

Whether it's a 5S implementation at Her Majesty Revenue and Custom (HMRC), a bank losing billions, GE saying it can't afford to do Six Sigma, the National Health Service (NHS), insurance companies, service companies or manufacturing organizations, regardless of market sector, size of company or stage of development, it sometimes seems as if everyone and his dog is doing something with a TPS (Toyota Production System) derived product, and finding it just as hard to sustain success today as they did 30 years ago following the introduction of Quality Circles and Total Quality Management (TQM). The billion dollar question has to be, why?

The Emperor and the townspeople did not share what they knew with one another. Although organizations today likely have their own tales of comparable absurdity, they have access to a wide variety of tools and strategies to enable information sharing. For the Emperor, it is unlikely that such structural elements as an intranet, expert network, or the position of a Chief Knowledge Officer would have helped him gain the critical information that he needed. Greater attention to the behavioural norms would likely have saved the Emperor from such enormous embarrassment, and sometimes in business life we have access to excessive and conflicting information. Simple technology, such as a mirror, actually existed for the Emperor and still works in the 21th century. If you see yourself naked in the mirror, you should believe what you see. You do not need a new management fad or an expensive consultant to tell you that you are naked.

In their efforts to increase information sharing, organizations will want to consider the insights in this book on the use of fair process, profiting from mistakes, and fostering a sense of organizational ownership. Hopefully, practitioners will be prompted to develop their own strategies that enhance information sharing so that learning can take place and knowledge can be created. It is fortunate for us today that, while the challenges of information sharing still remain, significant progress has been made in our understanding.

Management fads are like clothes. Maybe you don't really need new clothes? Changing clothes all the time for the whim of fashion can be a costly exercise. Asking the right questions does not make you stupid or incompetent. Outside the world of fairy tales, more people in today's organizations should be brave like the child in the fairytale. If you see that the Emperor is naked, you should tell him upfront!

Chapter 5: Dealing with the Emperor's New Clothes

Hans Christian Andersen's story of "The Emperor's New Clothes" is one of the earliest known accounts of a trick that some technology salespeople use all the time. Let us first recap the story, and then we'll explain the trick and how we propose to deal with it.

The Plot of the Children's Story

According to the plot, a pretentious emperor always wants to be seen as superior to everyone else. Some con men convince him that they can make him a new set of clothes that are better than anything he has ever worn. The clothes are incredibly thin and luxurious, and so light that they feel like air. But the clothes have one interesting property; people who are unworthy cannot see them at all.

So the con men get out their weaving equipment and go through the motions of making cloth. The emperor watches the early stages of manufacture, and notices that he can't see the cloth. But he keeps his mouth shut because speaking out would reveal the emperor as unworthy. The con men continue with their charade, pretending to sew the invisible cloth together until they have an invisible set of clothes.

The con men bring their fake clothes to the emperor in his bedroom. The emperor strips down, and the con men pantomime putting the clothes over the emperor's head and fastening them in place. "Are they not as light as air, just as we promised?" they ask. The emperor is too proud to admit that he cannot see anything, and agrees that they are definitely very light.

The emperor gets in his open carriage for a trip through the city. The story of the emperor's clothes has preceded the procession so everyone watching the king figures that they must be unworthy, because they cannot see anything. No one watching the procession wants to acknowledge this, because then everyone would know that they are unworthy. But then a small child cries out, "The emperor has no clothes!" Suddenly everyone, including the emperor, realizes that they have been conned.

The Modern Trick

The modern equivalent of this trick are efforts to sell a technology that doesn't make sense by convincing you that the technology is so advanced that you cannot understand it. The sales people start with a simple yet far-reaching premise. It usually goes something like this; "We have invented a revolutionary new database technology that will completely eliminate fraud by providing full traceability of all transactions back to their original source." The target audience for the sales presentation is a group of senior executives in a company that has recently been victim of fraud or, even better, a group of senior executives who work for a competitor of the victim. The executives in the actual victim company will be more suspicious, but their competitors will be naive and yet eager to prevent a similar problem in their own company.

The salespeople schedule a meeting with the executives in the company. IT people are included, but they are outnumbered by operational executives with limited technical background. The Chief Information Officer (CIO) will probably bring along one or two database experts, just to make sure there is technology expertise around the table.

The presentation begins. The first part of the presentation attempts to scare the hell out of the audience, reeling off one horror story after the next about fraud and the cost to its victims. Statistics are cited to make it seem likely that there is no way to escape this problem; it will hit you sooner or later no matter what you do. If it happens to you there are no excuses since a simple technology can easily prevent such wrongdoings.

Next come some complicated diagrams and charts which explain the new innovation. To a non-technology person they look impressive. They are full of technical terms that are vaguely reminiscent of other technical words that have been thrown around a little bit by your IT department; things like relational database, multi-phase commit, fault-tolerance, multi-threading, and maybe even that most sacred of all current technology terms, "the cloud!"

The appeal of the presentation is emotional, not logical. The salespeople want you to see their software as the only true solution to a problem that is infecting the entire world. Given the heavy executive weighting of the audience, it is unlikely that the company's technology experts will get much opportunity to ask questions. But if they do, the salespeople are well prepared with answers that sound good to the executives but don't actually address any of the real technical issues. The unspoken message to the technical people is, "this technology is so advanced that we don't expect a mere mortal like you to understand it. But believe me, it works." You don't want to appear stupid or incompetent and therefore you don't object, or proclaim that "the Emperor is naked."

By the end of the presentation, the executives are ready to sign up. The discussion is not about accepting or rejecting the sale, but instead about how fast the technology can be implemented. The CIO and the technical people know that there is too much momentum to stop this thing so they instead try to rein in the discussion, offering alternatives like a "proof of concept" or a "limited pilot."

And this is where the most important issue comes to the forefront; how much is the CIO trusted by the executives? If the trust is there, then the momentum of the sales pitch will be broken, and a more rational and proven approach will prevail. The CIO might assign someone to investigate this technology further, the IT organization will gather information from reputable technology assessment firms, and a team will talk with current customers using the technology to get a feel for the real cost/benefit ratio it offers.

But if the trust between the business and IT isn't there, then there is a 90% chance that some form of contract will be signed before the end of the week. Some number of months later, the poor CIO will be put in the unenviable position of having to explain to the business executives why this miracle technology could not deliver the promised results for their business. And there is a very good chance that the CIO won't survive in the job another year. After all, if a miracle is promised and it is not delivered, then whose fault is it? It must be the CIO who didn't implement it correctly, since it obviously couldn't be the technology!

Lessons from the Parable

1. If a concept cannot be explained simply, don't buy it. Good products are sometimes complex, but there is no magic to them. Every good yet complex product has a simple explanation for its effectiveness that is understandable to any knowledgeable buyer. Put your vendors on the spot: Ask them for that simple explanation. And if they cannot provide an acceptable answer, then throw the vendor out.
2. There are a lot of reasons why it is important to have trust between your business executives and your IT executives. The non-technical executives should have someone they can trust with technical decisions. If that trust is not there, then you are going to have technical decisions made by non-technical people, which is never a good thing.
3. Don't let the business buy a product whose only advantage is high technology if your own technology people don't fully agree with the premise.
4. If something sounds too good to be true, it probably is!

Although our example is an "advanced" database technology, we have seen this trick used equally effectively by some people selling Customer Relationship Management (CRM) systems, Enterprise Resource Planning (ERP) systems, cloud solutions, and even accounting software. In each case the salespeople promise a magic solution but fail to disclose all of the behind-the-scenes hard work and changes in business processes that are required to successfully implement the new system. Even the best products have no magic bullet; the computer systems are just doing something that you could do manually, but the systems are doing it more reliably and millions of times faster. Ultimately it is not the product that produces the good result; it is the changes you make in your business processes to support the product. Don't let your business people forget that. New so-called smart technology inventions are sometimes as "magnificent" as the Emperor's New Clothes.

Quotes:
"The new field force management system was presented as the new miracle of the century. Two years into the implementation it still does not work as promised. We would have been better off using the old simple Excel based system." (Sales Director of a FTSE 250 company)

"It all sounded too good at the outset. What we got out of it was yet another IT system that does not link to our many other ad-hoc systems. It just added to our current spaghetti set-up of incompatible systems." (Finance Manager)

"Treating an individual patient, I often have to go into 4-5 different databases during a normal working day; I spent more than one hour going in and out of the various systems. Individually the systems deliver what they promised to deliver but they don't talk to each other." (Danish Hospital Doctor)

Chapter 6: Examples of Failed IT Projects

There are of course numerous successful IT projects, but this chapter will show a non-exhaustive list of notable project failures. As you go through it you will observe that project failure happens in every industry and in every geographical location. However, we concentrated on IT project failures in this chapter for the sake of simplicity and to make our points. Both private and public companies suffer as a result of failed projects. Companies and agencies sometimes do everything possible to hide failed projects and since lessons aren't learned, the vicious circle is not broken and new projects suffer the same fate. Below is a "Catalogue of Catastrophe," a table of failed or troubled IT projects from around the world.

Catalogue of Catastrophe				
Company Name	Project Type	Project Name	Date	Cost
J.P. Morgan Chase & Co.	Financial risk analysis tool	New Synthetic Credit VaR (Value at Risk) Model	Sep 2011 (project) – Apr-Jun 2012 (operational failure)	Approximately $6B
British Sky Broadcasting (BSkyB) Limited – Middlesex, UK	Customer Relations Management system	Sky CRM Project	Jan 2010 court case concluded	£265M
Marin County - California, USA	Enterprise Resource Planning system – Accounting package	MERIT (Marin Enterprise Resource Integrated Technology)	Jan 2013 court case settled	$33M

Catalogue of Catastrophe				
Company Name	Project Type	Project Name	Date	Cost
State of California – California, USA	Payroll and benefits system	21st Century Project MyCalPAYS	Feb-13	$254M
US Department of Defence – U.S. Air Force	Integrated supply chain and logistics system	Expeditionary Combat Support System (ECSS)	Nov-12	$1B
2012 Mitt Romney Presidential Campaign – USA	Orca	Political campaign – Operations management system	Nov-12	Unknown
Fox-Meyer Drug - USA	Enterprise Resource Planning	Unknown	Aug 1996 (filed under golden oldies)	$40B write down in share value – company bankrupt
London Stock Exchange - UK	Share trading system	Taurus (Transfer and Automated Registration of Un-certificated Stock)	Mar 1993 (filed under golden oldies)	£75M lost by the London Stock Exchange and as much as £400M by other stakeholders
British Home Office - UK	Mobile computing implementation	Mobile Information Programme (MIP)	May-12	£103M

Source: Computerworld.com.

It is obvious that projects fail for many reasons. Everyone working on a project has his own opinion about the ultimate causes of its failure. It is impossible to have two completely identical failed projects with the same scope, objective and unexpected situations. However, knowing the causes of one project failure provides an opportunity to avoid pitfalls in future projects.

Should you be concerned about all of the potential reasons for project failure?

Remember the story of "The Emperor's New Clothes;" when his clothes were completed, the Emperor paraded through town to show them off. All the townspeople pretended to admire his new clothes until a young child exclaimed, "But he hasn't got any clothes on!" And then the whole town realises this and shouts, "But he hasn't got any clothes on!"

The Emperor had a creepy feeling down his spine, because it began to dawn on him that the people were right. "All the same," he thought to himself, "I've got to go through with it as long as the procession lasts." So he drew himself up and held his head higher than before and the courtiers held on to the train that wasn't there at all (Hans Christian Andersen, 1837).

Is this too common in your work environment? Have you ever dared to say that the Emperor is naked? The earlier you dare to proclaim it, the earlier "the procession" can come to an end.

Food for thought!

Quote:
"We knew early on that the IT project would be a failure, however we had already invested too much resource into the project and management did not want to lose face." (Manager, FMG Company).

Chapter 7: Leadership Lessons from the Emperor's New Clothes

Childhood is full of stories that are passed down from one generation to another. These stories often allow tired parents to both lull their high-energy kids to sleep and teach them a life lesson. Like most children, we loved to hear our parents tell us these stories (even if we did not always get the life lesson). There was that one story, however, The Emperor's New Clothes, that made no sense to us as a child and never put us to sleep!

Every time we heard this story of the naked emperor walking around his kingdom, we would ask the following:
- Why was the emperor so easily fooled by others?
- Why did all of the adults in the story refuse to tell the emperor the obvious?
- Why did only a child have the courage to speak the truth?

With time, we came to understand the story. Leaders impact the behaviour of those who follow them. The Emperor's New Clothes is a valuable parable on the failure of leadership that teaches the following four lessons:

1. Insecure leaders hurt the business enterprise. Some leaders have an excessive need for

recognition and praise. Other leaders care too much about what others think of them. These leaders hurt the business enterprise because they divert organizational resources towards the wrong outcome; their own ego needs. True leaders inspire others to follow them to fulfil strategic goals. These goals meet the needs of the business, not the leader's needs.

2. Leaders have to create the right environment for honest communication to occur. To get honest communication from organizational stakeholders, leaders have to recognize and reward those individuals who speak honestly. Leaders also must be open to criticism of their own efforts. Effective leaders learn to focus on the value in the message, not on the messenger. They are not threatened by disagreement or criticism. They encourage both to get the best results for the business.

3. Leaders need self awareness. We all have our strengths and weaknesses and this is true of the best leaders as well. Leaders need to be self-aware and understand their areas of weakness, emotional triggers, and the skill areas where they need the assistance of others. Effective leaders are self-aware and they have emotional intelligence. No matter how smart they may be, effective leaders know their limitations.

4. Leaders need to surround themselves with the right people. Leaders need smart, skilled people working for them who speak their conviction, help the leader avoid poor decisions, and provide expertise that supplements the leader's own skills and abilities. Effective leaders create an environment that fosters motivation.

Ultimately, the story of the emperor is the tale of an insecure leader who was unable to develop beyond his shortcomings. Effective leaders are seldom born. They evolve over time. They develop their skills, learn from their mistakes, focus on the strategic needs of the organization, and develop "a tough skin."

Chapter 8: Employee Engagement

Considering its much touted potential, it's no wonder that empowerment receives all the attention it does. Who wouldn't want more highly motivated employees to help scale the twenty-first century? As one CEO said, "No vision, no strategy can be achieved without able and empowered employees."

Top-level executives accept their responsibilities to try to develop empowered employees. Human resource professionals devise impressive theories of internal motivation. Experts teach change management. Executives themselves launch any number of programs from reengineering to continuous improvement to Total Quality Management (TQM). But little of it works.

Take reengineering for instance. Although the rhetoric of reengineering is consistent with empowerment, in reality it is anything but that. Both research and practice indicate that the best results of reengineering occur when jobs are rigorously specified and not when individuals are left to define them. Even the GE workout sessions had their greatest success when they addressed problems that were relatively routine. Reengineering has led to improvements in performance, but it has not produced the number of highly motivated employees needed to ensure consistently high-performing organizations.

Few executives would deny that there has been little growth in empowerment over the last 30 years. The reasons for this lack of growth remain a riddle with a complex answer. The change programs and practices we employ are full of inner contradictions that cripple innovation, motivation, and drive. At the same time, CEOs subtly undermine empowerment. Managers love empowerment in theory, but the command and control model is what they trust and know best. For their part, employees are often ambivalent about empowerment; it is great as long as they are not held personally accountable. Even the change professionals often stifle empowerment. Thus, despite all the best efforts that have gone into fostering empowerment, it remains very much like the emperor's new clothes; we praise it loudly in public and ask ourselves privately why we can't see it. There has been no transformation in the workforce or a sweeping metamorphosis.

To understand why there has been no transformation, we need to begin with commitment. Commitment is not simply a human relations concept. It is an idea that is fundamental to our thinking about economics, strategy, financial governance, information technology, and operations. Commitment is about generating human energy and activating the human mind. Without it, the implementation of any new initiative or idea is seriously compromised. According to Argyris (1998), human beings can commit themselves in two fundamentally different ways - externally and internally. Both are valuable in the work-place, but only internal commitment reinforces empowerment.

1. **External commitment:** Think of it as contractual compliance; it is what an organization gets when workers have little control over their destinies. It is a fundamental truth of human nature and psychology that the less power people have to shape their lives, the less commitment they will have. When, for example, management single-handedly defines work conditions for employees, the employees will almost certainly be externally committed. That commitment is external because all that is left for employees is to do what is expected of them. The

employees will not feel responsible for the way the situation itself is defined. How can they? They played no part in the defining.

2. **Internal Commitment:** If management wants employees to take more responsibility for their own destiny, it must encourage the development of internal commitment. As the name implies, internal commitment comes largely from within. Individuals are committed to a particular project, person, or program based on their own reasons or motivations. By definition, internal commitment is participatory and very closely allied with empowerment. The more that top management wants internal commitment from its employees, the more it must try to involve employees in defining work objectives, specifying how to achieve them, and setting stretching targets. The job needs to have the right blend of challenge, variety, importance and autonomy.

We might well ask whether everyone must participate in order for empowerment to exist in an organization. In principle, the answer is "yes" in reality, there is a "but". It is unrealistic to expect management to allow thousands of employees to participate fully in self-governance. The degree to which internal commitment is plausible in any organization is certainly limited. Moreover, the extent of participation in corporate goals and aspirations will vary with each employee's wishes and intentions. Nevertheless, the responsibility for such participation is on the emperor, or the top management!

In today's business world it's the responsibility of top management to convey the sense of purpose of the organization and how that links to the daily work of the individual employees. Employees have a legitimate need to feel they are part of the organisation. Many CEOs are so preoccupied with quarterly survival, in an attempt to satisfy shareholders and in certain instances themselves, that they fail to tell their employees a convincing and memorable fairy tale about the sense of purpose in the organization and the long-term future of the corporation. Today's corporate world needs much better storytellers. We believe storytelling can be a powerful tool to connect employees to top management's ideas and help the employees to make sense of the world around them. Fairy tales and stories stick. Lengthy, technical and colourful PowerPoint presentations don't. At best they occupy space in your computer's hard disk, or, to use the modern term, cloud storage!

Quotes

"The sales target was given to me top-down. They should have involved me as I am the one that understands the market. How can I be committed to a target I don't believe in?" (Country Manager of a FTSE 250 Company)

"Our CEO presented more than 30 slides about our Plan to Win. To me it was very technical and I am not sure I fully understood where he was coming from. But I dared not say that. Maybe it is only me being stupid." (Manager at a FTSE 250 Company)

Chapter 9: Variety of Employee Enabling Activities

Hopefully our advice in this book is not another version of "The Emperor's New Clothes." It is an outcome of studying relevant management literature coupled with our hands-on experiences as practising managers. Following on from the previous chapter, if you are looking for real advice about people management your goal should be to create a work environment in which people are empowered, productive, contributing, and happy. Don't hobble them by limiting their tools or information. Trust them to do the right thing. Get out of their way and watch them flourish! Then they will make a difference.

Below are variety of enabling activities for managing people in a way that reinforces employee empowerment, accomplishment, and contribution. These management actions should in our opinion enable both the people who work with you and the people who report to you to thrive.

1. **Demonstrate that you Value People**

Your regard for people shines through in all of your actions and words. Your facial expression, your body language, and your words express what you are thinking about the people who report to you.

Your goal is to demonstrate your appreciation for each person's unique values and talents. No matter how an employee is performing on his or her current task, your value for the employee as a human being should never falter and always be visible and expressed.

2. Share Leadership Vision

Help people feel that they are part of something bigger than themselves and their individual job. Do this by making sure they know and have access to the organization's overall mission, vision, and strategic plans. Tell the story like a fairy-tale make it as short and simple as possible.

3. Share Goals and Direction

Share the most important goals and directions for your group. Where possible, make progress on goals measurable and observable and ascertain that you have shared your picture of a positive outcome with the people responsible for accomplishing the results. If you share a picture and share meaning, you have agreed upon what constitutes a successful and acceptable deliverable. Empowered employees can then chart their course without close supervision. You should know the end and the moral of your shared fairy tale from the outset.

4. Trust People

Trust is the core of any fruitful relationship. Trust is also closely correlated with time and money. If trust decreases, the time and costs for implementing a given project increase. Conversely, if trust goes up, the time and costs for any project go down. Trust the intentions of your people to do the right thing, make the right decision, and make choices that may not be exactly what you would decide yourself. Nonetheless, if it works, acknowledge it and praise your people.

When employees receive clear expectations from their manager, they relax and trust the manager. They focus their energy on accomplishing instead of wondering, worrying, and second-guessing.

5. Provide Information for Decision Making

Make certain that you have provided people with, or make sure that they have access to, all of the information they need to make insightful decisions.

6. Delegate Authority and Impact Opportunities, Not Just More Work

Don't just delegate the drudge work; delegate some of the fun stuff, too. Delegate the important meetings, the committee memberships that influence product development and decision making, and the projects that people and customers notice. The employee will grow and develop new skills. Your plate will be less full so you can concentrate on contribution. Your reporting staff will gratefully shine and so will you.

7. Provide Frequent Feedback

Provide frequent feedback so that people know how they are doing. Sometimes, the purpose of feedback is reward and recognition as well as improvement coaching. People deserve your constructive feedback, too, so they can continue to develop their knowledge and skills.

8. **Solve Problems - Don't Pinpoint Problem People**

When a problem occurs, ask what is wrong with the work system that caused the people to fail, not what is wrong with the people. Worst case response to problems is to seek to identify and punish the guilty.

9. **Listen to Learn and Ask Questions to Provide Guidance**

Provide a space in which people will communicate by listening to them and asking them questions. Guide by asking questions, not by telling grown up people what to do. People generally know the right answers if they have the opportunity to produce them. When an employee brings you a problem to solve, ask, "What do you think you should do to solve this problem?" Or, ask, "What measures do you recommend we take?" Employees can demonstrate what they know and grow in the process. Eventually, you will feel comfortable telling the employee that he or she need not ask you about similar situations. You trust their judgment, and by having your employee finding the solutions themselves, your own life will often be easier and more fulfilling.

10. **Help Employees Feel Rewarded and Recognized for Empowered Behaviour**

When employees feel under-compensated, under-titled for the responsibilities they take on, under-noticed, under-praised, and under-appreciated, don't expect results from employee empowerment. The basic needs of employees must feel fulfilled for employees to give you their discretionary energy, that extra effort that people voluntarily invest in work. Recognition plays a significant role in successful employee empowerment.

Monetary rewards will not do the job alone. A simple recognition in the form of a "Thank You" in front of peers can often be extremely motivating.

Interview with the CEO of a very successful FTSE 250 Company

The CEO explained the five employee enabling activities steps used in his organisation to Empower Employees.

He said: "Without a strong belief in employee empowerment and clearly defined steps to help guide self-direction, our customers might not have experienced the successful on-the-spot solutions provided by the empowered employees. I believe firmly in encouraging employees to take initiative, to responsibly provide solutions that answer customers' challenges, and to do what is necessary to ensure customer satisfaction."

Below are the answers to the five questions we asked our guest CEO.

1. **Do your employees easily take responsibility?**

Not all employees want to make a decision. Some would rather let a co-worker or manager handle all issues, afraid that making the wrong decision could come back to haunt them. In order to encourage these hesitant employees to take steps forward, it is important to ensure that wrong decisions are not punished. It is also important to ask those employees what they think. Once they feel comfortable being part of the solution by offering suggestions that are not dismissed, they will feel ready to take charge.

2. Do you clearly communicate why empowered employee actions are so important?

Communication is key. We make sure that everyone understands the big picture and knows the reason for the specific needs and actions that affect the customer's experience. If someone only gets information on a need-to-know basis and does not understand the bigger picture, you eliminate the possibility of creating new ideas and new solutions. If that feeling pervades the work environment, it prevents people from feeling included.

3. Do you use real-life examples of empowerment as training tools?

Much can be learned from reviewing decisions made by an employee who provided a successful customer solution. Good examples provide real-life case studies to share as educational tools. Examples of actions that could have been improved provide a great opportunity to bring the employee and a group of peers together to discuss other options that could have been taken to achieve the same result. Not all departments can apply a blanket policy of empowerment, so being able and willing to customize training by departments gives employees a stronger sense of best practices.

4. **Do you restrict your employees' power to make decisions?**

Empowering employees is all about making a challenging situation for a customer or client better. You cannot limit actions with restrictions and expect to get the same results. Obviously, confidence and training is required but ultimately employees want to be a part of a success story. If you give them the room and guidelines to make quick decisions, a customer's dissatisfaction can turn into an exceptional experience.

5. **Do your employees feel like they are a real part of the entire organization?**

If not, a management philosophy enhanced by employee empowerment will be difficult to implement. Employees need to feel they are integral to the success of the overall business. By giving them the freedom and comfort of knowing they can contribute by action or suggestion, you help build a culture that reflects today's workplace needs.

Food for thought; maybe not all Emperors are naked!

Chapter 10: Information Sharing

The story of "The Emperor's New Clothes" illustrates the clear distinction between what we know and what we share. The story has prompted this chapter, in which we review significant real-life stories and present a model of a culture that we believe enables and encourages information sharing.

Additionally, we review key behavioural norms that we believe encourage information sharing, including the use of fair process to build trust, being open to disclosing and capitalizing on mistakes, and fostering a sense of joint ownership of work products. This chapter provides the practicing manager with specific examples and suggestions for implementing information sharing.

While one of the authors was reading Hans Christian Andersen's "The Emperor's New Clothes" to his five-year-old daughter, he saw that the story was in many ways about information sharing. It describes, in an exaggerated way, some common reasons why people in organizations do not share what they know.

You may remember that the tale is about an emperor with a very singular interest in clothes. He takes no interest in his soldiers, the theatre, or driving about in his state coach, unless it is to show off his new clothes. One day two swindlers arrive in town who know how to weave the most magnificent fabric that can be imagined. And more amazingly, clothes made of the material are invisible to everyone who is either unfit for his post or inexcusably stupid. The Emperor thinks this is useful, because he will now discover who is wise and who is foolish. So, he gives the swindlers large sums of money, fine silk and gold thread and they pretend to weave a beautiful fabric.

The Emperor wants to find out how the work is proceeding. Uneasy about going himself in case he is unable to see the cloth, the Emperor sends his Chamberlain who he is certain is wise and well suited for his position. Hiding his panic when he is unable to see the material, the Chamberlain feigns admiration and listens carefully to the description provided by the swindlers. The Chamberlain then returns to the Emperor and repeats the swindlers' description. And so the tale goes on, with other people pretending to see the cloth and sharing what they pretend to see with the Emperor and one another.

When the clothes were completed, the Emperor paraded through town to show them off. All the townspeople pretended to admire his new clothes until a young child exclaimed, "But he hasn't got any clothes on!" And then the whole town shouted, "But he hasn't got any clothes on!"

The Emperor had a creepy feeling down his spine, because it began to dawn on him that the people were right. "All the same," he thought to himself, "I've got to go through with it as long as the procession lasts." So he drew himself up and held his head higher than before and the courtiers held on to the train that wasn't there at all (Hans Christian Andersen, 1837).

You might remember, as a child, thinking that everyone in the story was very silly. As an adult, the characters feel less silly and uncomfortably familiar. Many people identify with the anxiety and fear of the Chamberlain and others as they wonder if they are stupid or unfit. Many also identify with the overwhelming need to hide this fact so as not to be exposed. The most uncomfortable part of the story for some is the concluding description of the Emperor. Everyone knows that he is only wearing his underwear and deep down he knows it too. But he believes that the only way to preserve dignity and avoid embarrassment is to pretend that he does not know what he knows.

This story illustrates the very clear distinction between what we know and what we share. The story also illustrates two forces that encourage us to separate what we know and what we share: self-interest and the fear of exposure. We will discuss those cultural factors, both structurally and behaviourally, which enable practitioners to foster information sharing in an organization.

The topic of "knowledge management" has received a great deal of attention in contemporary management literature. O'Dell and Grayson (1998), define knowledge management as the "conscious strategy of getting the right knowledge to the right people at the right time and helping people share and put information into action in ways that strive to improve organizational performance."

We have observed that the majority of today's companies are using knowledge management programs and plan to increase these efforts over the coming years. Interest in knowledge management is often rooted in the view that we are living in what is called a "knowledge economy," where the ability to acquire and apply knowledge is the key competitive advantage. Managers everywhere are seeking to leverage individual and group knowledge by sharing it throughout an organization. A critical component of knowledge management initiatives is getting employees to share information.

This strong interest in knowledge management is also based on new opportunities to share information across complex and global organizations provided by advances in technology. Technology plays a fundamental role in knowledge management and the sociological aspects of knowledge management need to be integrated with the technological. This combination creates a cohesive philosophy and strategy for developing an organization's capabilities to generate and share knowledge. Technology is very effective for information sharing. However, the socio/technical approach is vital to information sharing. Texaco's knowledge management guru John Old (2001) says:

"Any technology solution will fail if it doesn't recognize the importance of human connections. Here at Texaco, our strategy is to connect people and help them leverage their know-how. Knowledge is contextual, so technology that simply enables people to 'write down what they know' doesn't work very well. And you can't force people to share knowledge."

A review of the definition of "knowledge," however, makes it clear that the term "knowledge sharing" is an oxymoron. The Merriam Webster Dictionary defines knowledge as "understanding gained by actual experience." This suggests that knowledge cannot be transmitted, but can only be gained through reflection on action. The fact that by definition only information, not knowledge, can be shared among individuals who do not share a common context and experience has significant implications for knowledge management.

Another challenge in today's' business world is the overload of information. We have experienced that in many corporations, total "e-mail anarchy" exists where everybody presses "Reply to All" to almost everything. In that way everybody's aunt and uncle are involved in everything! Without proper e-mail discipline the "Sender" drowns the "Recipient" in unnecessary information and indirectly steals his or her valuable time. Many managers talked about receiving 100 to 300 e-mails per day. Nobody can deal with that much information in a meaningful way. Imagine if proper discipline could reduce the number of e-mails by, say, 50%, or outlook could have a warning pop-up window before anybody could send an e-mail to a mass audience. "Are you sure you really need to send this e-mail to all the chosen recipients?"

Information sharing presents practical and conceptual challenges. Information sharing is one of the most difficult aspects of a knowledge management program. As the tale "The Emperor's New Clothes" describes, what people know and what people share are often quite different. In many organizations the tendency is for people not to share.

Quotes

C. Douglass Izard (2003), Director of Tax Knowledge Management at KPMG Peat Marwick, explains, "It is a big cultural change for a professional-services firm to share, because people in the past were rewarded for not sharing knowledge."

"You built an expertise in a certain area, and that is how you made a lot of money; by performing that for clients, not by sharing it across the firm." (Master, 1999).

Below is example of good intentions, but little information sharing at a medical device company.

Quotes

"We have a team meeting every morning at 8:00AM. Initially, these meetings were very quiet. Lee and I (Roger) did most of the talking. John would add a comment or two as appropriate, but the rest of the group only spoke when they were spoken to. Lee worked on drawing input from the silent majority. Sometimes he was successful, sometimes not. I got the impression the new members of the group were afraid to say something stupid. They were very ill at ease, often fidgeting while Lee and I discussed more technical issues. I knew, and I am sure Lee did too, that they generally had no idea what we were talking about. In this period of time, Lee took the communicator role, and I generally played the contributor. Sometimes I would switch to the challenger role. This role was especially important as

Lee was inexperienced both as a supervisor and at the plant. I felt it was important to establish our goals and standards from the start. We would only have one beginning. I wanted to do things right."

Roger shows that Lee and him are well intentioned but little interaction occurs among other team members. The adjective "quiet" is not a good sign. Any information sharing initiative must overcome this preference for not sharing.

Therefore, in the corporate world we believe we need more brave Children who dare to say that the Emperor is naked. Being factual and upfront can often save time and resources, as well as speed up the right decisions. Next time you are faced with daily situations resembling "The Emperor's New Clothes" help yourself, your colleagues and the company by saying you see him as naked. At least the people who have read this book will know what you mean and everybody will get a good, healthy and relieving laugh. And everybody in the Board room will echo you: "Yes, he actually is naked."

Chapter 11: Using Fair Process to Build Trust

The principal theme of this chapter is that in our opinion lack of engagement with employees of an organisation is a huge, unrecognised problem. Listen to your employees. If not it results in lack of trust in senior management (to make good decisions or act with integrity) and impacts negatively on the overall motivation. The good news is, however, that executives can build processes to try to build trust. One strong method is to involve employees in, and make transparent, decision processes. Under those circumstances, employees will even commit to management decisions and strategies; even if they do not agree with it; if they believe the process has been fair and transparent.

The analogy we like is of a woman receiving an unfair parking ticket. She was determined to go to court and fight the fine. However, on her arrival the judge dismissed the case without even hearing it and she was allowed to leave with no fine. Instead of being thrilled that she had got off (and without even a fight), she was furious and frustrated that she had not received "justice." So although she liked the outcome, she did not like the process and ended up unhappy.

Economists assume that we are rational people who are focussed on outputs and this assumption has been built into management tools, such as incentive systems and organisational structures. We human beings are not that simple and we actually do care about the process as well. This is particularly important in the knowledge economy, where value creation depends upon ideas, innovation and information sharing. A fair process allows managers to achieve difficult and painful goals while gaining voluntary cooperation. Without a fair process and its open implementation, even simple goals are tough to reach.

Below are our suggested three simple principles of Fair Process.

Engagement: Involving individuals in the decisions that affect them by asking for inputs and allowing them to refute the merits of one another's ideas and assumptions. It communicates management's respect for individuals and their ideas. Encouraging refutation sharpens everyone's thinking and builds collective and institutional wisdom. Engagement results in better decisions by management and greater commitment from all involved in executing those decisions.

Explanation: Where everyone involved should understand why final decisions are made as they are. Explanations make people confident that decisions were made impartially and in the best interests of the company.

Expectation: Clarity where once a decision has been made, managers state the new rules of the game. Employees must know by what standards they will be judged and the consequences of failures. To achieve a fair process, it matters less what the new policies and rules are and more that they are clearly understood. Happy employees!

Taken together, these three principles collectively lead to a fair process. This is crucial as any subset of the three will not result in the open and visible implementation of a fair process.

A critical point is that a fair process does not mean attempting to make decisions by consensus and does not seek to make everyone happy. What it does is give every idea a chance to be put forward for approval or rejection based on its merits. It does not mean that managers forfeit their right to make decisions or have to run some type of democratic process. The decision still lies in the hands of the management team; they are simply able to select the best option no matter where it came from or how many people put it forward.

If a fair process policy has to be put in place because of a reaction from employees, it is almost too late. The organised protest will probably be looking for a fair process and retribution on those that did not demonstrate it previously. They will probably also be insisting on detailed and often inflexible processes to ensure that a fair process is used in the future; such is the emotional power that an unfair process can provoke. Therefore managers who view a fair process as a limitation on their freedom or resent that they need to gain input from their employees need to be aware that the retribution that they might face is likely to be far more painful than the cost of implementing a fair process. Partly in recognition of this need for a fair process, combined with the critical fact that maximisation of the brainpower and ideas of your staff is a high value-creating activity.

Quotes:

"We knew the new incentive scheme would become a failure. Many of us had tried the chosen approach in our previous jobs. They could at least have engaged us and we would never have had to implement such a de-motivating scheme." (Sales Rep of a FTSE 250 Company)

"The big firing round made everybody in the department nervous. If they had at least explained to us why 10 of our colleagues had to leave, we would still not have liked it but at least we would have understood why and we would to a greater extent have accepted the situation." (Product Manager, FMG Company).

Chapter 12: Using Mistakes as an Opportunity for Learning

Sharing best practices usually focuses on learning from and duplicating what has been done right. A more difficult goal of information sharing initiatives is to learn from mistakes, because a common behavioural norm is that people only prefer to share information associated with positive outcomes. This norm is perhaps another way to think about the behaviour in "The Emperor's New Clothes." No one wants to be the bearer of bad news to the Emperor, to tell him that he is a victim of fraud and finally that he is wearing no clothes.

Looking at our interpretation of the tale and drawing parallels to our practical management experiences, it is particularly difficult to share negative information which you perceive as reflecting on your own shortcomings. A widely held view that errors are indicative of incompetence leads people in organizational hierarchies to suppress mistakes and deny responsibility. Organizational norms and systems, however, can affect attitudes and behaviours toward errors. In a recent case of errors in hospital administration of medication in the UK, a non-punitive environment was essential to uncovering and dealing with errors productively. Because the behavioural norm is to hide mistakes, organizations need to encourage the sharing of mistakes as well as successes.

In the example below, we contrast the negative atmosphere of "make no mistakes" to the positive climate of recognizing that "mistakes will happen" as we learn new skills.

It is All Right to Make Mistake

The concept of empowerment to improve staff motivation and confidence is validated by one of the authors' personal experience.

"Several years ago our plant began a process of significant organizational changes. These changes came about abruptly and with little notification. In addition, upper level management became extremely authoritarian. The result was that the entire site, myself included, was in a state of powerlessness. Productivity came to a standstill as people were afraid to make mistake. I felt I had no participation in my future or control of my situation. With productivity at an all-time low, a new resident Managing Director was brought in to take over. He took immediate steps to correct the situation, including personally expressing his confidence in the plant staff. He made it known that it was all right to make a mistake. The results were immediate; people were determined to get the station back on line. This is not to say that this solved all of our problems at our plant. But with renewed motivation and confidence, other problems became solvable."

Because the easiest kinds of mistakes to detect are ones of commission, punitive organizations can create an environment where the sensible choice is not to do anything. Organizations most often decline not due to errors in what they did, but in what they failed to do, or lost opportunities. For example, it can be argued that IBM's decline in the 1980's was because they missed the mini-computer revolution.

Of course we don't endorse any mistake for the sake of organizational learning. When it comes to ethical business practises, health and safety there is zero tolerance for mistakes, however, a story from a good friend of ours at a UK car manufacturing plant provides a contrast to the experience above.

The management policy at this car manufacturing plant has been verbatim compliance with procedures. Because procedures cannot be written with every contingency, they are often incomplete, contradictory and inaccurate. The management attitude regarding procedure adherence had in the past been short-sighted. Workers who mindlessly followed incorrect procedures which caused negative results received disciplinary action. Likewise if workers who did not follow the approved procedures and made it more efficient and were found out, they were also subject to disciplinary action; a catch 22!

Another behavioural norm is that individuals are most likely to share with others who are interdependent to them in order to coordinate their activities to achieve goals. The natural sharing that occurs from interdependent work is the glue within communities of practice. When acting alone, simple self-interest can predict behaviour. I help you if you help me; I don't help you if you don't help me. Creating interdependence is more of a structural than a cultural issue. But the social and organizational context can influence the dynamics of interdependent relationships.

It is unclear whether the Emperor in the fairy tale was learning from his mistakes – the answer is obviously not. However, our experience from real life shows that those organizations, which allow mistakes and learn from those mistakes, create a much more positive learning environment.

Chapter 13: Learning from Children

In our society we are taught to be ashamed of mistakes. We are all imperfect. What we need to achieve is the courage to change our debilitating beliefs about imperfection. This is one of the most encouraging concepts, and yet one of the hardest to achieve in the business world and in our society as a whole. There isn't a perfect human being in the world, yet everyone is demanding it of themselves and others.

Close your eyes and remember the messages you received from parents and teachers about mistakes when you were a child.

What were those messages?

To make this exercise more powerful, you may want to write them down. When you made a mistake, did you receive the message that you were stupid, inadequate, bad, a disappointment and a klutz? Close your eyes again and let yourself remember a specific time when you were being berated for a mistake.

What were you deciding about yourself and about what to do in the future?

Remember, you were not aware that you were making a decision at the time, but when you look back those decisions are usually obvious. Some people decide they are bad or inadequate. Others decide they should not take risks for fear of humiliation if their efforts fall short of perfection. As discussed above, too many decide to become approval junkies and try to please their boss at great cost to their self-esteem. And some decide they will be sneaky about their mistakes and do everything they can to avoid getting caught.

Are these healthy messages and decisions that encourage productive life skill development?

In our mind, of course not. When parents and teachers give children negative messages about mistakes, they usually mean well. They are trying to motivate children to do better for their own good. They haven't taken time to think about the long term results of their methods. So much parenting and teaching is based on fear.

Adults fear that they are not doing a good job if they do not make their children do better. Too many are more concerned about what the neighbours will think than about what their children are learning. Others are afraid that children will never learn to do better if they do not instil in them a sense of fear and humiliation related to mistakes. Most are afraid because they do not know what else to do and fear that if they don't inflict blame, shame and pain, they will be acting permissively. Often adults cover up their fear by exerting more control over their children.

There is another way. It is not permissive, and it truly motivates children to do better without paying the price of a lowered sense of self-worth. We need to learn and teach children to be excited about mistakes as opportunities to learn.

Wouldn't it be wonderful to hear an adult say to a child, "You made a mistake? That is fantastic. What can we learn from it?"

And "we" does really mean "we." We are partners in many of the mistakes made by children. Many mistakes are made because we haven't taken the time to train and encourage our children. We often provoke rebellion instead of inspiring improvement. Model the courage to accept imperfection so that children will learn from you that mistakes truly are an opportunity to learn.

Many families have found it helpful to invite everyone to share a mistake of the day and what they learned from it during dinner time. Once a week during a class meeting, some teachers allow time for every student to share a mistake and discuss what they learned from it. Children need daily exposure to the value of mistakes and learning from them in a safe environment.

The Three Rs of Recovery from Mistakes
1. Recognize-- "Wow! I made a mistake."
2. Reconcile-- "I apologize."
3. Resolve-- "Let's work on a solution together."

It is much easier to take responsibility for a mistake when it is seen as a learning opportunity rather than something bad. If we see mistakes as bad, we tend to feel inadequate and discouraged and may become defensive, evasive, judgmental, or critical of ourselves or others. On the other hand, when mistakes are seen as opportunities to learn, recognizing them will seem like an exciting venture: "I wonder what I will learn from this one." Self-forgiveness is an important element of the first R of Recovery.

Have you ever noticed how forgiving children are when we are willing to apologize?

Have you ever said you were sorry to a child? If so, how did that child respond?

We ask this question at every opportunity all over the world, and the response is universal. When adults sincerely apologize, children always say, "That's okay, Mum" (or Dad, or Teacher). Children can be feeling angry and resentful in response to disrespectful behaviour one minute (and adults probably deserve it) and switch to total forgiveness as soon as the adult says, "I am sorry."

The first two Rs of Recovery, Recognize and Reconcile, create a connection before the third R, working on solutions. Trying to work on solutions before creating a connection is entirely unproductive.

Just like most adults and children, even when we know better, we do not always do what we know is the right thing to do. As human beings, it is common for us to become emotionally hooked and lose our common sense. We revert to our reptilian brains, and reptiles eat their young. We then thoughtlessly react instead of acting thoughtfully. One thing we love about the Positive Discipline principles is that no matter how many mistakes we make and no matter how many messes we create with our mistakes, we can always go back to the principles, learn from our mistakes, clean up the mess we made and make things better than they were before the mistakes.

Since we make so many mistakes, the Three Rs of Recovery is one of our favourite concepts. Our signature example is the time one of the authors said to his fifteen-year-old son, "Karl, you are a spoiled brat." (Does that sound like kindness, firmness, dignity, and respect?)

Karl, who is very familiar with the Three Rs of Recovery, retorted, "Well, don't tell me later that you are sorry."

In total reaction, the father said, "You don't have to worry, because I am not." Karl ran to his bedroom and slammed the door. The father soon reverted back to his rational brain, realized what he had done, and went to his bedroom to apologize to Karl. He was still angry, and was not ready for an apology. Karl had his copy of an early edition of Positive Discipline and was very busy underlining with a big, black marking pen. The father looked over his shoulder and saw that Karl had scribbled "phony" in the column.

The father left the room thinking, "Oh dear, there will probably be another Mummy Dearest book hitting the market any day." He knew he had made a huge mistake.

In about five minutes Karl came to the father, timidly putting his arms around him and said, "I am sorry, Dad."

The father said, "Honey, I am sorry too. In fact, when I called you a spoiled brat, I was being one. I was upset at you for losing control of your behaviour, but

I had lost control of my own behaviour. I am so sorry."

Karl said, "That is okay, I was acting like a brat." The father responded, "Well, I can see what I did to provoke you to act that way."

Karl said, "Well, I can see what I did." We have seen this happen over and over. When adults take responsibility for what they did to create a conflict (and, any conflict takes at least two) children are usually willing to follow this modelling and take responsibility for their part.

Children learn accountability when they have models of accountability. A few days later the father overheard Karl on the phone saying to his friend, "Oh Aston, you are so stupid!" Karl quickly realized what he had done and said, "I am sorry Aston. When I call you stupid, that means I am being stupid."

Karl had internalized the principles of Recovery and learned that mistakes are nothing more than wonderful opportunities to learn.

Our illustrative example of the father and his son is not so different from what we experience on a daily basis in business life as we observe the interaction between managers and their subordinates.

We wonder if the Emperor learned from his mistake!

Chapter 14: Avoid the Dangers of Management Babbles

One of the problems with cubicle life, especially for those in big corporations who find themselves promoted closer to one of those offices with a window, is that sometimes the higher up the corporate ladder you climb the more out of touch you seem to sound. Instead of using plain English you start jabbering abstract nonsense about "leveraging brand equity," "creating touch points" and "engaging super-users." Most of the young professionals these days prefer the word Strategic in their job titles. Director of something "strategic" sounds pretty sexy!

The strategy word is to us one of the most misused words in today's business world. Everybody talks about it and has a strategy for this, that and the other, but very few can actually articulate what they mean. To us it is pretty simple. Before even starting to discuss strategy you need to decide precisely what it is you are after, i.e. your goal. Strategy, in essence, is then about selecting and identifying a pattern of activities that will maximize your chances of reaching your specific goal. To make the point, if you want to grow your business 10% over the next 5 years you need to identify and select a certain pattern of activities that will be quite different from a situation, where your goal is to keep the business flat for the next 5 years.

Lengthy PowerPoint presentations, motivational slogans of the month and long lists of initiatives and priorities are common features of corporate communication, but after sitting through a meeting filled with them one realizes that they are just babble. Once the presentation is over or the slogans are memorized, are people really going to work harder or motivated to do anything differently? No, because what is said in those meetings does not effectively communicate exactly what the leaders want to be done and often instead just adds more confusion. These communication outlets are overcomplicated, and, while they do list specific strategies to reach objectives, they do not speak plainly about how the employees himself/herself can work to achieve those objectives.

This chapter focuses on ways to cut through all of the corporate babble and to plainly say what the business strategies actually ask of the employees and for the employee to hopefully have the courage to let the Emperor know whether he is wearing any clothes!

Babble is any type of communication that does not actually direct the employees after they hear it, or time wasting activities like motivational meetings that no one ultimately takes anything away from.

What we are suggesting is a strategy to streamline communication within an organization so the employees can fully understand what management is trying to say. The approach is to simplify communication and cut through the clutter of the typical corporate communication methods. We encourage leaders to break down the broad or confusing corporate objectives into the main actions the leaders want their employees to take; actions that will lead to reaching those objectives. For example, saying, "increase customer satisfaction to 98 percent," is difficult for employees to determine what actions are needed to reach that goal, and instead leaders should say, "always treat customers with respect and do your best to help them." The effects of that behaviour will lead to the desired results. Employees can more effectively follow objectives and reach company goals when they can clearly understand what they are being asked to do.

Our suggested approach is founded on the Action Equation of know + feel = do, meaning, "what people know, plus what they feel, inspires them to take the right actions to execute strategy."

We would like to suggest that leaders decide on a couple of main objectives that they need their employees to follow and that will inspire their desired improvements. Limiting the selection of priorities is based on the idea that people focus well on a handful of priorities, but they lose their way if the list is too long. We have seen employees having 10-15 detailed objectives, clearly following the SMART principles (Specific, Measurable, Achievable, Relevant, Time bound). On paper and with the best intentions, review cycles are established (setting objectives, mid-year evaluation and year-end review. On paper it all sounds right. It is in line with what we learned at our MBA schools and everybody praises the concept. However, often we have seen a lot of the Emperor's New Clothes in this area. Reality often does not follow the text book and the principles are not at all carried through in daily practice outside the academic world. Nobody dares to say he is naked. That would make you look stupid and incompetent.

Managers should find out what motivates their employees to work at their best performance level and use that passion to drive their productivity. We encourage managers to look at their extensive corporate strategies and break them down into simple instructions to clearly state what it is that they actually want done so employees are no longer confused by what direction their work should focus on.

The simplistic approach to management on strategy is to combine ideas from collaborative management with Management by Objective (MBO) strategies. The collaborative management approach emphasizes leadership and decision-making as a continuing process, and in on strategy communication leaders are constantly enforcing the main principles they want their employees to remember when they are working. Once the few main objectives are met and performance is improving, then managers can add more objectives and it becomes a building process. Leaders are also encouraged to include employees in the decision-making process. As leaders develop their plans, it is clearly in their best interest to enable employees to participate in strategy development and decisions about execution. This allows the employees to feel more connected to the strategy and to know how to best carry out their own individual goals and objectives.

The main management theory this model follows is the MBO approach. We continuously encourage leaders to cut through the babble and convey the main goals that need to be reached to their employees, while not confusing them with complicated business strategies that follow the MBO strategy of having employees focus on results. This streamlines the thought process of the workers and allows them to confidently make decisions on how to best work toward their company's objectives. Also, MBO has five management roles, and two of those, setting objectives and motivating and communicating to employees, correlate with the on strategy approach. Objectives are supposed to be reasonable and simple so employees can easily remember them, which is exactly the point we are making. To reiterate, SIMPLIFY and limit the number of objectives.

We hope the message of simple and concise communications we are trying to promote resonate with our readers. Leaders' careers should be based on his or her ability to effectively communicate, and we hope this chapter illustrates the difference between what a leader says and what the employees hear, as there can be a large disparity between the two. The advice we offer is that leaders should think of the main points of their business strategy and focus on communicating them in the most straightforward way. This will make employees more likely to remember what is asked of them and therefore help achieve the company's objectives. For managers it should be like telling a fairy tale. The story needs to have a beginning and end and a clear moral. However the story should be credible and everybody should be able to see that the Emperor is not naked.

Quote:
"I am not sure I fully understand the long-term strategy of the company. Where are we going in the next 5 years? Where will it all end? The Managing Director said we all have to contribute to the future success. Honestly I am not sure exactly what I am supposed to do. All the strategy talk was pretty fluffy." (Sales Manger, Fast Moving Goods)

Chapter 15: All Good Fairy Tales Come to an End with a Memorable Moral

We would like to conclude by saying that "The Emperor's New Clothes offers us a heads-up and invites us to exhibit the best traits of human nature!"

The story started with two travelling rogues who scheme to make lots of money by capitalizing on the vanity of the Emperor. This Emperor loves clothes and would change them often, admire himself and demand that others do the same. The "tailors" gain an audience with the Emperor by saying that after years of work they have discovered a way to make a fabric so light and fine that it is almost invisible. As a matter of fact, it is so light that stupid and incompetent people cannot see it at all. The Emperor is easily convinced and pays them a fortune to weave this cloth and tailor it into a kingly outfit.

After a while, the Prime Minister is sent to report on their progress. When he is shown the cloth he of course sees nothing. He breaks out in a sweat, fearing that the worst is true about his stupidity and incompetence. To hide this terrible truth, he praises the beauty of the cloth to the tailors and then the Emperor. The tailors appear with the bolt of imaginary cloth to show the Emperor who, like the Prime Minister, hides the fact that he too must be stupid and incompetent by declaring the cloth beautiful. It is then tailored into an outfit that the Emperor tries on. All present admire the beauty of the cloth and beg the Emperor to show it to his subjects. The Emperor is a little squeamish about this but is reassured that only the stupid among them will not see its beauty.

The two tailors hold his imaginary train as he begins the parade. The people are eager to see the cloth but also to see which of their neighbours are too stupid and incompetent to see it. Of course, they are dismayed when they cannot see it for themselves. As a result, all declare it to be a beautiful outfit. But there is a child among them with no important job or position to protect, who declares, "But he's naked!" The father tries to hush the child, but it is too late. The word spreads and finally all acknowledge that the king is naked. The king waddles his way, head held high, back to his castle.

So what does the story suggest we watch for in the workplace?

1) The two scoundrels display behaviour motivated by self-centeredness and deceit. Their desire for wealth leads the two to behave in any way needed to get it. Their values go out of the window as they use dishonesty to take advantage of the Emperor's weakness to get what they want. They are not citizens of the kingdom and if they ruin reputations or damage relationships to attain their goal, it is of no concern because their focus is on what they want alone and if they are lucky, they will be gone before the impact of their dishonesty is discovered. Does this ring a bell?

Lesson: Be a team player. By definition, being a team member means we sacrifice our individual needs and preferences for the good of the whole. Differences of opinion are natural and become the grist for creative discussion. Holding our positions is important for our own integrity and the decision-making process but must be balanced with the flow of that process, the effectiveness of the group, and our future relationships with our team members. Once made, the team's decision must be supported by all team members in all venues regardless of their position on the issue during the process. Conflict and commit. All need to weigh in during the discussion with their true opinion but then, once a decision is made, all must commit to it privately and publicly.

2) The Emperor shows us vanity and the resulting abuse of his leadership position. The Emperor is fixated on his appearance and changes clothes many times a day. The thrill of each new outfit and the recognition that results lasts only for a while and so his need for more attention and self-admiration is insatiable. It is his vanity that the two "tailors" capitalize on to manipulate the Emperor. The Emperor's ego is at the centre of the kingdom and his court knows that if they want to keep their position they had better serve it well.

Lesson: Leadership is service. While the Emperor has position, he is not a leader. He has substituted the appearance of kingliness for the function of genuine leadership. Our egos create the blind spots that others see and must deal with because we do not. It is essential to create enough safety so trusted others can give us the feedback needed to protect the quality of our leadership from personal blind spots. And, like the Emperor, we need to remember that the success of our leadership is based not on others serving us but on our serving of others and our organizations.

3) The Prime Minister and the subjects show us the impact of judgment and criticism. They fear being judged and seen as stupid and incompetent. They are absorbed in this fear of what others might think and, fearing that they could be right, deny their experience

of reality that "the Emperor is naked;" they say whatever they think will sound good to others. Because they fear judgment themselves, they take pleasure in the opportunity to confirm their neighbour's stupidity.

Lesson: Create safety. The fear of judgment is a powerful driver that can take over the culture of a department, team, or company. If this dynamic and the fear it creates is not eliminated, surviving it will become the goal and people will focus on what they think others want to hear rather than what needs to be said. Reality gets lost and the ridiculous becomes the norm. If you see this happening; do some exploring. Find out whose ego is being protected or what people are afraid of. Then refer to the lesson below.

4) The child shows us the freedom to speak the truth that comes when we are not attached to any particular outcome and are fearless. He makes no judgment about the Emperor's nakedness; he just states that he is naked. One small statement of reality spreads like wildfire because it has the power of truth behind it. This gives others the freedom to deal with the reality their fear previously caused them to deny.

Lesson: Be courageous! The child has nothing to lose and so can afford to be fearless in his description of the Emperor. Most of us have something to lose and so can find it tough to be literally fearless. We need courage instead. Courage is being afraid of what is in front of you and taking a step towards it anyway, which is much tougher than fearlessness. It is what we see heroes do on battlefields and shop floors, as fire fighters and as managers, in conference rooms and kitchens. Life offers each of us the opportunity to be heroic by telling and being willing to hear the truth a little more each day.

So "The Emperor's New Clothes" is not just about the foibles of leadership. It has lessons for us all.
- Be courageous and speak up
- Be a team player.
- Leadership is service.
- Create safety.

We are all surrounded by "the finest solutions to our challenges." Consultants and experts are ready to step in and help the Government, CEOs and Top Managers. They normally show them a repository of the best references from companies and Counties they have helped so far. Why do Governments, CEOs and Top Managers need "weavers" to make it right? What are their motives for engaging expensive consultants and experts? Do they not know the answers themselves or do they just need consultants to justify decisions they have already made? Do they need consultants to identify the "incompetent and stupid" parts of their organizations?

We hope this book provided useful answers to some of the above questions and you as the reader could draw parallels to "The Emperor's New Clothes" in your day-to-day corporate or personal life.

Other Book from the same Authors

You can get a copy of Paperback and Audio Version of this book from Amazon.com, iTunes Store and any other major book stores including University Libraries worldwide.

www.ingramcontent.com/pod-product-compliance
Lightning Source LLC
Chambersburg PA
CBHW072038190526
45165CB00018B/1084